Spies and Spying

SPY
TECHNOLOGY

Stephen Timblin

A+

Smart Apple Media

Smart Apple Media
P.O. Box 3263, Mankato, MN 56002

Printed in the United States of America

Library of Congress Cataloging-in-Publication Data

Timblin, Stephen.
  Spy technology / Stephen Timblin.
      p. cm. -- (Spies and spying)
  Includes index.
  ISBN 978-1-59920-361-4 (hardcover)
  1. Espionage--Technological innovations--Juvenile literature. 2. Espionage--History--Juvenile literature. 3. Spies--History--Juvenile
literature. 4. Spies--Biography--Juvenile literature. I. Title.
  JF1525.I6T56 2010
  681'.76--dc22

                                                                                                                2008049280

Created by Q2AMedia
Editor: Honor Head
Art Director: Rahul Dhiman
Designer: Ranjan Singh
Picture Researcher: Shreya Sharma
Line Artist: Sibi N. Devasia
Coloring Artist: Mahender Kumar

All words in **bold** can be found in the glossary on pages 30–31.

9 8 7 6 5 4 3 2 1

CONTENTS

SPY TECHNOLOGY

A spy without gadgets is like a doctor without tools: both know how to get the job done, but the chances that their operations will succeed are not very good.

Tools of the Trade

Spies have to keep one step ahead of the enemy. That is why technology is so important. Spies need the most up-to-date camera and recording equipment to get the information, and radios and codes to send the secrets back to base. If spies get caught, they need something slick and quick to use to defend themselves.

A talented spy learns how to blend in with the shadows.

Cameras need to be small and silent—the click of a camera could easily give this spy away.

A Spy's Life

Gadgets alone won't make a spy great. To be successful, spies need to stay cool in hot situations, be ready to operate on short notice, and live a double life in secret. They also have to know their gadgets. Just like that doctor, if a spy can't use his gadgets properly, the outcome could be deadly.

Top Secret

Some secrets are more secret than others. Few people might be allowed to see secret files, but they might not be able to look at "Top Secret" ones. Other secrets may be labeled "For Your Eyes Only," meaning you can't show the document to anyone else!

SPY FILE

Baker the Faker

Lafayette Baker was a spy for the Union Army during the Civil War. He disguised himself as a photographer to get behind Confederate lines. He was caught after the enemy uncovered the fact that his camera didn't work!

EYE SPY

Cameras are one of the most important items in a spy's bag of tricks. Because they are so important, the gadgets for taking secret photos and videos are always being improved.

Say Cheese!

Before **digital cameras**, spies relied on cameras that used film. That didn't stop their organizations from creating miniature cameras hidden in everything from belt buckles to handbags and books. One of the best was the Steinbeck ABC camera. Built into a watch, the camera let spies take up to six photos while checking the time.

With the Steinbeck ABC camera, it's always time to take a photo.

Top Secret

One of the best hidden cameras was a camera worn under an agent's shirt and tie. This camera took photographs through a lens disguised as a tiepin. To snap a photo, an agent just tapped a button hidden in the pocket of his pants.

Do You Copy?

Let's say you're a spy and your snooping has uncovered a stack of top-secret papers. If you steal them, the enemy will know the papers were found. The solution? Leave the papers behind but snap a photo of each page using a special "copy camera." Designed to take pictures of documents, copy cameras can be as big as a briefcase or as small as a pack of chewing gum. The Soviet Union's **KGB** once made a copy camera hidden in a book. All an agent had to do was roll the spine of the book over a document to copy it.

This camera was used during the Cold War by the East German State Security Ministry known as the Stasi. The camera takes pictures through a false button set on the camera lens. The camera was held in place on a waist belt hidden under a coat. A cable with a lens shutter release went from the camera into the user's pocket.

The Pumpkin Papers

American Whittaker Chambers (1901–1961) began as a spy for the Soviet Union but switched sides. In the 1940s, he helped capture a Soviet spy by handing over papers and film containing secret information. These items became known as the "Pumpkin Papers" because Chambers had hidden them inside a pumpkin.

T931759

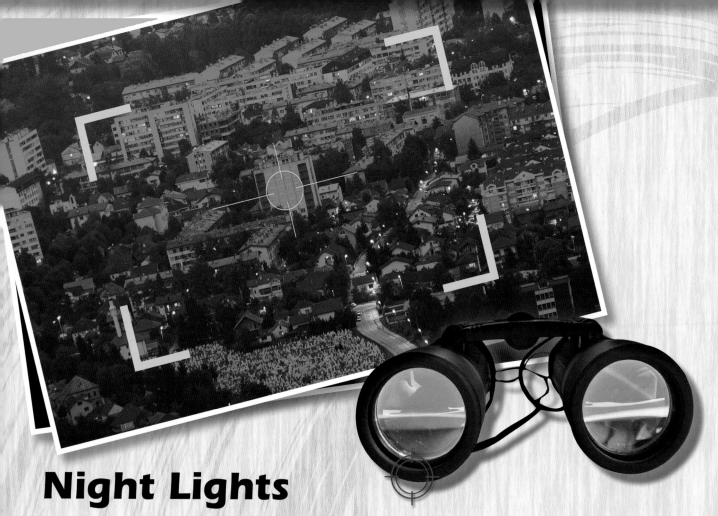

Night Lights

Spies have always used night-time to sneak around in secret. Now, with **night-vision goggles**, things have become much easier. Night-vision goggles work in two ways: some **magnify** bits of light that the human eye can't see, and others use **infrared** light to search for heat from warm bodies. In both cases, these high tech gadgets give spies the power to see and take photos, even on cloudy, moonless nights.

The dark of night is no longer safe for enemies with the development of night-vision technology.

Top Secret

The most famous spy camera is the palm-sized Minox. Invented by Walter Zapp in 1936, the minicamera silently takes up to 50 photographs. The Minox was so good that versions of it were used until the 1990s, when digital cameras came along.

Digital Days

Progress in computer technology has created a new range of cutting-edge digital cameras. Today, regular people have access to technologies that spies would love to have had ten years ago. One example is a video camera so small it can be hidden inside a teddy bear or wall clock. These cameras send their secret videos to recorders hidden in another room. The gadget, nicknamed Nanny Cam, is commonly used by parents to check their babies or babysitters.

Parents can keep an eye on their babies with a camera hidden inside a teddy bear.

BUG CONTROL!

Listening in secret to other people's conversations is an important way of getting hold of information. Years ago, agents had to risk physical danger to listen in. Today, spies can use bugs.

Hide and Speak

A spy can't always stick around to listen in on important conversations. That's why secret listening devices known as bugs were invented. By creeping into buildings and hiding bugs in key spots, spies can record conversations without being anywhere near the scene. Bugs are so small they can be hidden in everything from phones and pens to pieces of furniture.

A small bug is easily hidden inside a telephone.

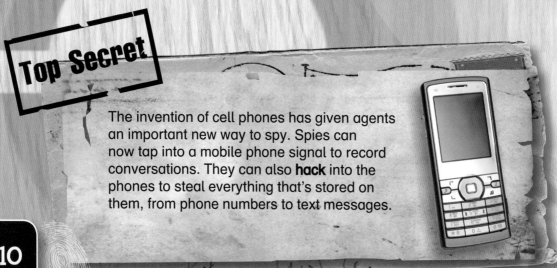

Top Secret

The invention of cell phones has given agents an important new way to spy. Spies can now tap into a mobile phone signal to record conversations. They can also **hack** into the phones to steal everything that's stored on them, from phone numbers to text messages.

The Man Without a Face

Markus Wolf (1923-2006) was the long-time leader of East Germany's HVA, a powerful secret service agency. He was known as the "man without a face" because he was never photographed until recently. Wolf's team of spies once placed so many bugs in the offices of Helmut Kohl, West Germany's leader, that Kohl had to use the public pay phones outside his office. Unfortunately for Kohl, Wolf had already bugged those phones too!

SPY FILE

Bug Alert!

Bug **detection** is just as important as planting bugs. Most bugs send information back using radio signals or infrared light. To search for bugs, spies **sweep** through rooms using anti-bugging devices that spot radio signals or the heat given off by bugs. High tech bugs can be turned on and off. This means agents need to search rooms carefully by hand for them before discussing secrets.

Watch what you say! In the 1970s, the CIA designed a watch that could record conversations.

A Surprise Gift

After World War II, the United States and the Soviet Union began a time known as the **Cold War**. For many years, the two nations spied on each other and prepared for a war that never happened. In 1946, the U.S. ambassador in Moscow, Averill Harriman, met with a group of Soviet schoolchildren who had a gift for him —a beautiful carving of the Great Seal of the United States. Harriman liked the wooden seal so much he hung it up in his office. What Harriman didn't know was that hidden within the Great Seal was a high tech bug!

The Great Seal of the United States. A gift that kept on giving secrets to the enemy!

"The Thing"

It was six years before the Great Seal listening device was discovered because it didn't use batteries or electric circuits. It was finally found in 1952, and experts nicknamed the tiny bug "The Thing" because they didn't know how it worked. A British scientist eventually realized the bug used radio beams and **vibrations** to pick up sounds. British and American spies made similar bugs to use against the Soviets!

Back of seal

Bug hidden inside seal

Hollow inside for bug

The front of the seal looked normal, but hidden inside was a dangerous secret!

Top Secret

The United States began building a new embassy in Moscow in 1979. Searches of the construction site found that spies had bugged the building. In fact, there were so many bugs that U.S. officials wanted the building torn down! Several floors had to be rebuilt, and it took until the year 2000 for the entire building to be considered safe.

Bug

13

BACK TALK

Getting top secret information is only part of a spy's job. Next, the spy has to send the information home without the enemy finding out.

Secret Codes

For thousands of years, codes have been used so that if enemies snatched messages they wouldn't be able to understand them. In the 1400s, an Italian named Leon Alberti invented a system called a **cipher** that created codes by mixing up letters of the alphabet. A century later, another Italian, named Giovanni Battista Porta, created **invisible inks**. One of the best was an invisible ink written on the shells of hard-boiled eggs. The secret messages could be read by peeling the egg to discover the writing on the white of the egg.

To crack a cipher code, you need an identical cipher such as this set up in exactly the same way.

A cipher wheel like this mixes up letters and numbers to make coded messages.

SPY FILE

Code Talkers

The U.S. Marines used an unusual "code" during World War II: the Native-American Navajo language. As the language had so few speakers and no written alphabet, the Marines believed their enemies would never be able to translate messages spoken in Navajo. Dozens of Navajos served in the Marines as "code talkers," delivering instructions over military telephones in their native language. Their code was never broken.

You've Got Mail

Experts say that as many as 125 billion e-mails are sent around the world each day. That adds up to 25 e-mails a day for every person on the planet! **Counter intelligence** agencies have experts who use advanced computer programs nicknamed "spybots" to sort through as many suspicious e-mails as possible.

Top Secret

In the 1980s, agents working for East Germany's Ministry for State Security were given a secret writing kit. Inside the case were pens filled with special inks. The inks were only visible on the page when viewed with a special **ultraviolet** light.

OUT OF SIGHT

Throughout history spies have used technology to hide everything—from soldiers to the tiniest photos.

When is a Horse not a Horse?

In ancient times, the Greeks fought the Trojans outside the city of Troy. To enter the city, the Greeks came up with a clever plan. They built a giant wooden horse and left it outside the city walls. Convinced by a Greek spy that the horse was a gift, the Trojans rolled the horse into their city. But, hidden inside the horse were Greek soldiers! That night, the soldiers climbed out of the horse and opened the city gates for the Greek army. The Greeks won the war soon after.

The Greeks used a huge wooden horse to smuggle soldiers into the city of Troy.

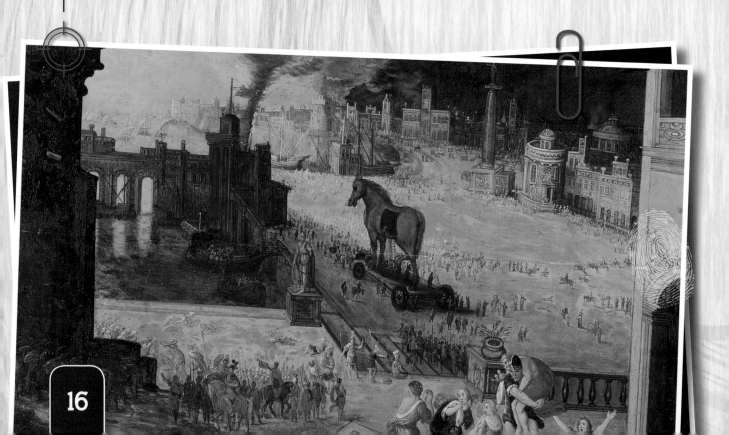

A coin can be hollowed out to hide microfilm containing important secrets.

Hidden Secrets

All sorts of everyday objects can hide secrets. During World War II, explosives were packed inside pieces of coal and then left on railroad tracks to blow up trains carrying supplies to the enemy. Shaving cream cans had secret compartments, a hairbrush had a camera hidden inside, and once even a piece of fake dog poop was used to hide messages!

Top Secret

Shoes have always been an important hiding place. They can have secret compartments for all kinds of equipment—such as small knives, or hidden microphones to record conversations.

Special Delivery

Secret agents often never meet face to face. Instead, to trade documents or money, they arrange what is called a **dead drop**. This means they leave items in a secret spot for the other agent to pick up later. These dead drops often use items like fake rocks or a hollow tree trunk with a compartment inside to hide the secret stash.

Dead drops for spies can be used and found anywhere.

Top Secret

FBI agent Robert Hanssen's job was to hack into computers to find spies, but Hanssen himself was a spy who sold secrets to Russia in exchange for cash and diamonds. He was arrested in 2001 while making a dead drop of classified documents under a bridge near the FBI's headquarters in Washington, D.C. He was arrested and imprisoned.

Micro Messages

To send messages a long distance, spies can use **microdots**. Created with special cameras, microdots are miniature photos that can pack a page of information into a space the size of a full stop. Agents receiving the microdots use a microscope to view the tiny photo. Microdots are so small they can be hidden under a stamp or even within a postcard picture before being mailed around the world.

SPY FILE

Secret Agent Trigon

Soviet diplomat Alexander Ogorodnik led a double life as a spy for the United States. Code-named "Trigon," Ogorodnik supplied the CIA with top secret documents in the 1970s. Always afraid of being captured by the KGB, he kept a deadly cyanide pill inside a pen built for him by the CIA. After being captured in 1977, Trigon swallowed the suicide pill to avoid being tortured during his KGB **interrogation**.

A single microdot is used to send coded information back to base.

WEAPON WONDERS

Part of a spy's job is to remain hidden. But if they get discovered—or if their mission calls for some action—they have to be ready for the worst.

Concealed Weapons

Clever scientists working in secret workshops make all kinds of weapons-in-disguise for spies. During World War II, tiny blades known as thumb knives were hidden in coins or sewn into the coat collars of British agents. These could be used to cut through ropes, slash enemy tires, or as weapons for self-defence.

These thumb knives may be tiny, but they can be deadly.

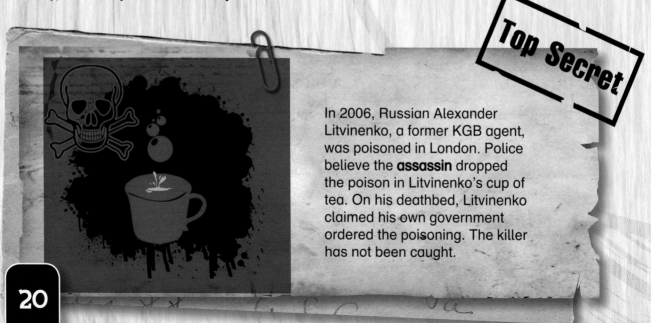

Top Secret

In 2006, Russian Alexander Litvinenko, a former KGB agent, was poisoned in London. Police believe the **assassin** dropped the poison in Litvinenko's cup of tea. On his deathbed, Litvinenko claimed his own government ordered the poisoning. The killer has not been caught.

Mighty Pens

Plenty of weapons have been hidden inside ordinary looking pens. Britain's **SOE** agency developed a pen that could shoot a single bullet and a deadly pen that launched a cloud of poison up to 6.5 feet (2 m) away. The KGB built several pens that could be used to assassinate enemies—one injected a pellet of poison into the victim, while another fired deadly hydrocyanic acid into the air.

This pen can launch a cloud of deadly gas.

SPY FILE

The Gadget Guru

A one-time commander of a nuclear attack submarine, Rolf Dietrich now builds the gadgets of the future for the U.S. **Homeland Security Department.** Some of his projects include remote-controlled planes built to protect airports from missile attacks, radiation-detecting cell phones, and even underwater bombs designed to stop hurricanes.

This poison pen can't write, but it can kill.

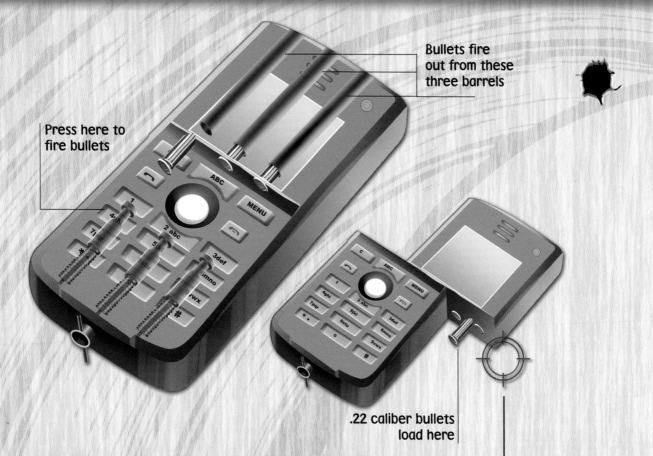

Bullets fire out from these three barrels

Press here to fire bullets

.22 caliber bullets load here

This looks like a cell phone, but it's actually a gun.

Hidden and Deadly

Agents cannot be seen carrying weapons, so clever disguises have to be created for them. During World War II, the U.S. Office of Naval Intelligence created a glove pistol that allowed a spy to deliver a punch and a gunshot at the same time. In the same war, British special operations agents wore belts that could fire a bullet out of the buckle. The Soviet Union's KGB were particularly clever at hiding guns. They invented a tube of lipstick and a flashlight that could fire bullets. The KGB's most daring creation was an umbrella that fired a poison pellet. In 1978, this weapon was used to assassinate the Bulgarian writer Georgi Markov as he walked across London's Waterloo Bridge.

Silent Killer

Firing a gun makes a lot of noise. For those times when a quiet shooting is needed, spies use a silencer. Also called suppressors, these devices fit onto the barrel of a gun and reduce the sound of a gunshot by up to 90 percent. Instead of a loud "bang," a gun with a silencer makes more of a soft "ping."

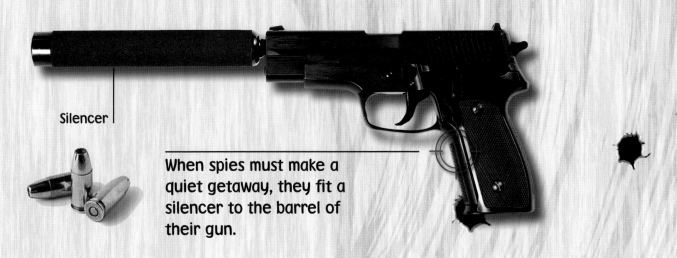

Silencer

When spies must make a quiet getaway, they fit a silencer to the barrel of their gun.

Top Secret

Not all spy weapons are disguised. The Walther PPK pistol has long been a favorite of agents around the world because it is small and reliable. The Walther PPK is the gun of choice for the fictional spy James Bond!

SPIES IN THE SKY

If you look up at the night sky, it's difficult to believe there are spying eyes in space looking right back at you. But space-age spying is now common around the world.

Balloon Platoon

In the U.S. Civil War, the Union Army used hot-air balloons on fact-finding missions. On September 24, 1861, a balloon called *The Union* rose more than 984 feet (300 m) into the air with Thaddeus Lowe as the pilot. Lowe sent information to Confederate troops on the ground by **telegraph**.

Civil War soldiers prepare to spy on the enemy by air.

The high altitude U-2 plane gives spies invisible eyes in the sky.

Seen and Unseen

The most famous spy plane is the U-2. It was designed by the U.S. military in the 1950s to spy on the Soviet Union. It could fly 13 miles (21,336 m) above the ground, and flew beyond radar range. Pilots used the planes to take photos of secret military bases. The U-2 was so well designed that newer versions of the plane are still used today.

SPY FILE

Crash Landing

On May 1, 1960, American pilot Francis Gary Powers (1929-1977) was shot down while flying a U-2 spy plane over the Soviet Union. A parachute landing saved his life. Powers was arrested soon after hitting the ground and put on trial in a case seen around the world. He was sentenced to prison, but the U.S. government traded him for a Soviet spy that they had captured.

Top Secret

First flown in 1964, the SR-71 Blackbird (right) holds the record for the fastest spy plane ever. It can travel at 2,193 miles per hour (3,529 km/h) and reach an altitude of up to 85,000 feet (25,908 m). At that height, it's almost impossible to shoot it down from the ground.

No Pilot? No Problem!

Some spy planes are unmanned. These pilot-free planes are called drones. One of the most popular drones is the Predator. A little less than 30 feet (9 m) long, this plane is used to spy on events close to ground. It can also fire deadly missiles at enemy targets. A larger drone is the Global Hawk spy plane, which can fly at altitudes of 60,000 feet (18,288 m) for 24 hours without refueling. The cameras and radars on the Global Hawk can see through clouds and sand storms.

An unmanned MQ-1 Predator sets off on a mission. Unmanned drones like these support ground forces with fire power, danger alerts, and reconnaissance (surveys of the enemy).

Hundreds of satellites circle the Earth daily.

Top Secret

To see how a spy might use a satellite image, go to earth.google.com. Type in your home address to see an image of where you live taken from space. The image won't be as detailed as those taken by government spy satellites, but it's still good enough to spot the important buildings in your area.

Space Spies

The first spy **satellite** was named Corona, and it was launched by the United States in 1960. After taking photos from space, Corona ejected its film with parachutes attached. Planes would then catch the floating film in midair. Modern satellites are far more advanced, but exactly how advanced is top secret. We do know that satellites today can clearly see an item the size of an apple from space. They can also track people within buildings by sensing their body heat.

CYBER SLEUTHS

From hacking into private networks to spreading a dangerous virus, the Internet is one of the main battlefields for spies in the 21st century.

Byte-Sized Bombs

The next big war could be a **cyber war**. The U.S. and British governments have released reports claiming that China has the tools to launch a cyber war. In fact, the **U.S. Congress** once called Chinese spying the "single greatest risk" to American technologies. A cyber war could include a country stealing important trade and business secrets. If hackers got enough information, they could steal vital military secrets and possibly even shut down the Internet completely.

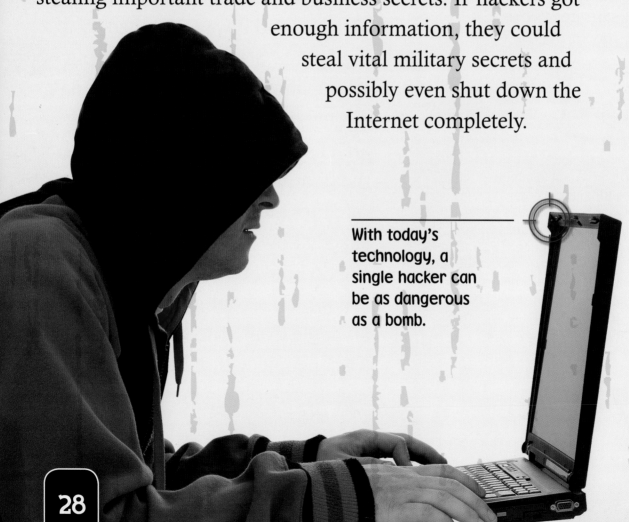

With today's technology, a single hacker can be as dangerous as a bomb.

Terror Online

Osama bin Laden, leader of the terrorist **al Qaeda** group, has long used the Internet to spread his message of violence. As part of their antiterrorist groups, both the CIA and FBI now have teams of computer experts who look for hidden images and messages on the Internet.

SPY FILE

Out of Sight

Spies use the Internet to send messages through steganography—hiding a message in plain sight. If you had a map to send to another spy, by using a special program you could "hide" that map in a vacation photo. Your contact could download the photo and then, using the same program, "unpack" the hidden map.

A **computer virus** is a program that enters a computer without permission. Viruses are deliberately sent to cause damage, or to wipe out information. They have been designed to infect millions of computers in a very short time. A virus could one day be used to attack another country's important computer networks.

Virus Warning

Top Secret

GLOSSARY

al Qaeda   an international terrorist organization led by Osama bin Laden from Saudi Arabia. It has a variety of goals, and these include ridding Muslim countries of any influence from the West.

assassin   someone who is paid to kill someone

CIA   the United State's Central Intelligence Agency

cipher   a system that creates codes

Cold War   the 1946–90 era of distrust between the United States and the Soviet Union

computer virus   a computer program designed to cause harm

counter intelligence gathering information on enemy spies

cyber war   a battle taking place over computer networks

dead drop   secretly exchanging items without meeting in person

detection   noticing or finding something hidden

digital camera   camera that stores images electronically and not on film

FBI   the United States' Federal Bureau of Investigation

gadget   device or tool

hack   to break into somebody's computer electronically

Homeland Security Department   U.S. agency created to protect the country against terrorist attacks and natural disasters

invisible ink an ink that only reappears when activated

infrared a range of light not visible with the human eye

interrogation questioning someone closely

KGB the Soviet Union's spy agency; stands for Komityet Gosudarstvennoy Bezopasnosti

magnify to make something look bigger

microdots tiny photographs used to hide messages

microfilm a way of taking and storing tiny photographs

night-vision goggles goggles that allow one to see in the dark

satellite an advanced machine placed into orbit around Earth

SOE a British group of spies during World War II

sweep to search a room for hidden objects

telegraph a system of transmitting information over long distances using radio signals

ultraviolet light a form of light not visible with the human eye

U.S. Congress a branch of the U.S. government responsible for creating laws

vibrations quick and typically tiny movements

INDEX

WEB FINDER

www.fbi.gov/fbikids.htm
The kids' page for the FBI includes games, a history of the agency, and adventure stories.

www.spymuseum.org/
Homepage for the International Spy Museum in Washington, D.C.